SPRING

It's quite sunny here with lots of green leaves. I've seen a baby rabbit. It's still raining a bit, but there's blossom on some of the trees.

See you soon!

SUMMER

It's really hot and hasn't rained for ages. There are lots of flowers, but the grass is looking dry. The fields are nearly ready for harvest.

See you soon!

AUTUMN

It's beautiful here! The trees have all sorts of red, orange and brown leaves. It's a bit wet and windy, so the leaves keep being blown off the trees.

WINTER

It's been cold for a while, but yesterday it started to snow! There aren't many wild animals about and hardly any flowers. Not many of the trees have leaves.

See you soon!

Write in the season:

1 Summer
2 Autumn
3 Winter
4 spring

Well done!

Why do we have day and night?

The Earth spins on its **axis** as it **orbits** (moves around) the Sun.

It's **daytime** when we face the Sun and **night-time** when we face away from it.

The equator is an imaginary line around the planet, dividing Earth into two hemispheres.

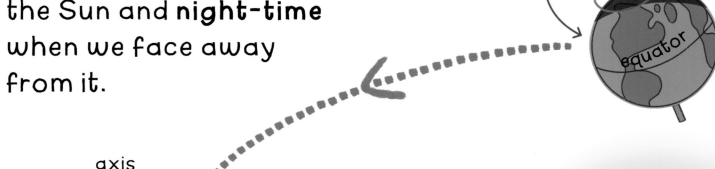

axis

direction of spin

winter in the northern hemisphere

summer in the southern hemisphere

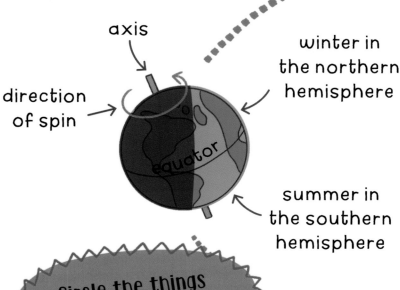

Circle the things you usually see in the **night-time.**

butterfly

Sun

moth

owl

stars

Moon

ANSWER: Moon, stars, moth, owl

Why do days change length?

The Earth is **tilted** as it spins. The part of the Earth that is tilted towards the Sun will have longer days – this is **summer**.

The parts that are tilted away are in **winter** and their days are shorter.

direction of orbit

summer in the northern hemisphere

equator

winter in the southern hemisphere

QUICK FACT!

At the North and South Pole, the days get so long in summer that there isn't any night-time at all!

Fill in the missing words, using the words 'winter' and 'summer'.

In July, it is _____ in the northern hemisphere and _____ in the south.

ANSWER: In July, it is summer in the northern hemisphere and winter in the south

Why does the weather change?

The tilt of the Earth also causes changes in the **weather** throughout the year. When one area of the Earth gets more **direct sunlight** than the rest, it warms up.

Finish the lines and **arrows** to show which part of the Earth is being warmed most by the Sun.

Sun

Earth

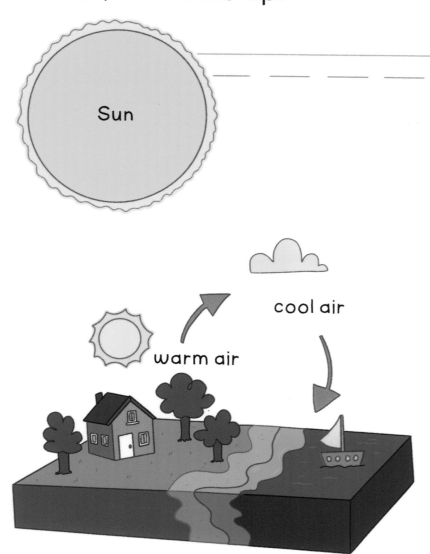

warm air

cool air

Warm air **expands** (takes up more space) so it becomes **lighter** and floats above colder air. When it **cools** down it becomes **heavier** again.

This causes **weather systems** to move around the world.

Scientists who study the weather are called **meteorologists**. They keep **records** of the weather every day.

cloudy

stormy

mixed

sunny

snowy

rainy

foggy

Keep a **weather** diary by filling in this chart each day. You could copy the **symbols** to help you.

	Monday	Tuesday	Wednesday	Thursday	Friday	Saturday	Sunday
Morning							
Afternoon							
Evening							

You can record the **weather** in a different **season**, just wipe this clean and start again!

Well done!

Winter

This is the **coldest** season with the **shortest** days of the year.

Many trees lose their leaves and in some places there is **snow** and **ice**.

As it's difficult to find food, some animals **hibernate** – a very deep sleep, where their breathing and heart rate slow down so they hardly need to eat.

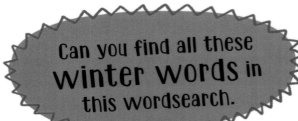

Can you find all these **winter words** in this wordsearch.

snow

cold

hibernate

migrate

ice

frost

e	n	w	f	h	s	u	r	x
l	t	o	r	s	n	h	n	b
p	o	m	o	c	o	l	d	r
i	m	i	s	k	w	b	f	n
c	d	y	t	q	l	c	x	s
e	t	z	h	v	x	i	f	y
x	m	i	g	r	a	t	e	l
q	r	r	t	q	h	b	o	w
h	i	b	e	r	n	a	t	e

Insects, birds and fish often **migrate** – travel somewhere **warmer** – for the winter.

Some animals like squirrels don't hibernate or migrate, but spend most of their time keeping warm in their **nests** and eating food they've **hidden** away.

Imagine if you had to stay in your bedroom for the whole winter. Draw the **provisions** you would need to have with you.

Precipitation

The scientific word for rain is **precipitation**. Snow, sleet and hail are all types of precipitation too – the water is just frozen!

The **water cycle** shows how **precipitation** falls, is collected, **evaporates** and **condenses**, before starting all over again.

CONDENSATION

As water vapour cools it condenses, turning back into tiny droplets of water.

PRECIPITATION

Water droplets in the clouds fall as rain, snow, sleet or hail.

EVAPORATION

The Sun heats up the water, so it evaporates into the air.

Draw arrows on the picture to show the direction of the **water cycle.**

COLLECTION

The water runs through rivers and streams, or soaks through the ground to end up back in the sea.

ANSWER: The water cycle is a constant cycle of precipitation, collection, evaporation and condensation

Meteorologists use a **rain gauge** to measure precipitation. It's important to know how much rain we have for farmers, water supplies and to predict future weather.

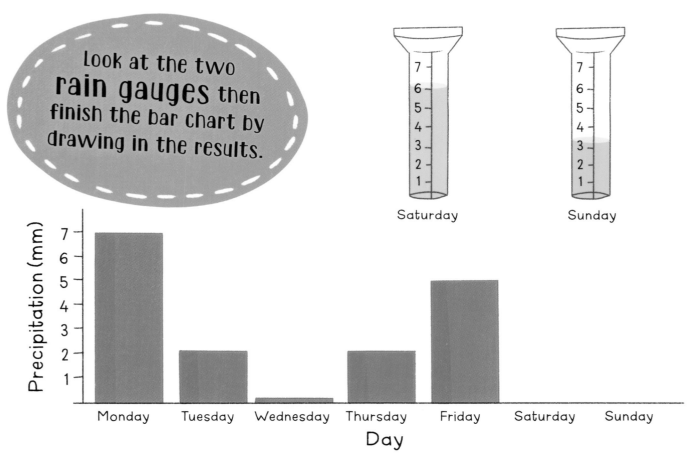

Look at the two **rain gauges** then finish the bar chart by drawing in the results.

Saturday

Sunday

Which day had the most rain?

Which day would be best for a picnic?

Why not make a **rain gauge**? Make sure you put a funnel in the top of the container to stop any rainwater from evaporating.

ANSWER: Monday had the most rain. Wednesday would be best for a picnic as there was very little rain

Well done!

Spring

This is the season for **new growth**. The weather is warmer and the days are longer. Seeds that have been in the ground all winter sprout **shoots**.

Things to look for in spring:

caterpillar

bluebells

bird's nest

new leaves

lamb

daffodil

frogspawn

This is what spring looks like where I live. Can you spot the things in the picture that tell us it is spring?

14

New leaves grow on the **trees** and spring **flowers** begin to grow. Hibernating **animals** wake up and animals that have migrated come back again.

Many animals have **babies** in the spring because there is a lot of food around.

What does **spring** look like where you live? What can you spot around your home?

My spring notes

Well done!

Summer

The weather is usually **warmest** in summer and the days are **longer** than the nights.

Most flowers **bloom** in summer and the trees are full of leaves, so there's **plenty of food** for insects. You can spot butterflies, ladybirds, bees and many other insects.

Follow the lines to find out which **butterfly** will reach which flower?

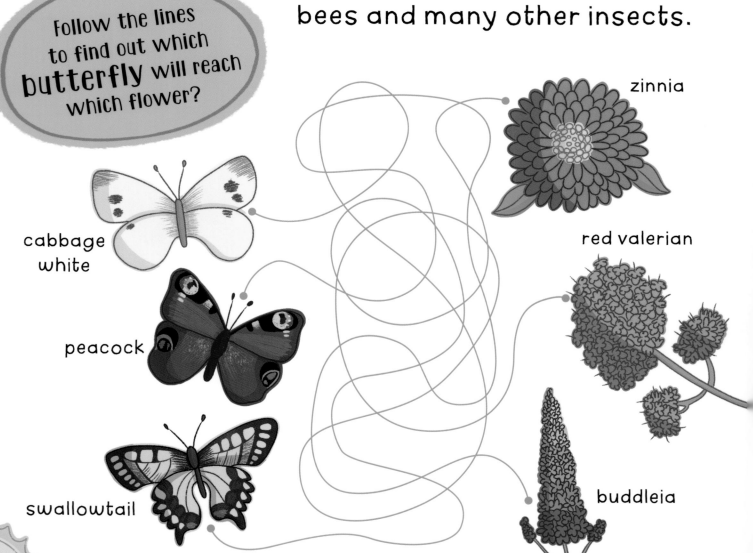

zinnia

cabbage white

red valerian

peacock

swallowtail

buddleia

Which food is in season?

Fruits and vegetables grow during **different seasons** in different countries.

To find out which food is in **season**, visit a market, shop or go online and look at the labels to see if it is grown locally.

Write down the fruits and vegetables that are **in season** where you live now.

Shopping list

_____ _____

_____ _____

_____ _____

Draw a picture of a delicious fruit or vegetable that grows in the summer.

Does it grow on a small plant, in the ground or on a tree?

_____

Well done!

Why do trees change colour?

Leaves contain a chemical called **chlorophyll**, which soaks up the Sun's energy to make food for the plant.

In winter, when there isn't much **sunshine**, some trees drop their leaves, then grow new, green leaves in spring. In autumn, the leaves will start to turn brown or red before falling off.

Trees that drop their leaves are called **deciduous trees**.

> Draw lines to match up the pictures of the trees to the correct **seasons**.

spring   summer   autumn   winter

ANSWER: From left: spring, winter, summer, autumn

Why do trees change colour?

Some trees keep their leaves all year round. These are **evergreen trees** and we can't tell what season it is by looking at them. Most plants change throughout the year by growing **new leaves**, **flowers** or **fruit**.

> Find your way through this maze, following the pictures in the correct seasonal cycle.

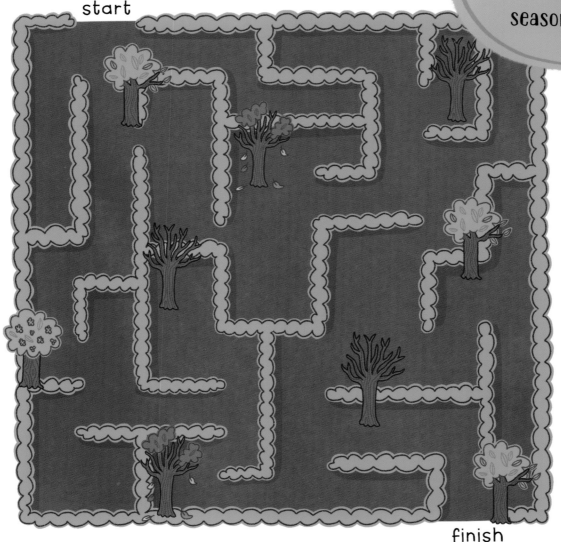

start

finish

Keep an eye on a plant where you live to see if it **changes** each season.

Well done!

Autumn

Autumn is a season full of different **colours**. Leaves on the trees turn red, yellow, orange and brown and begin to fall off to help the tree conserve water and energy.

Things to look for in autumn:

birds flying south

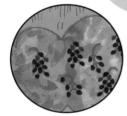
blackberries

caterpillar cocoon

animals ready to hibernate

toadstools

harvesting

This is what autumn looks like where I live. Can you spot the things in the picture that tell us it is autumn?

Some animals **store** food for the winter or will get ready to **hibernate** or **migrate**.

Autumn is a busy time for farmers; **harvesting** and making the fields ready for next year's crops.

What does **autumn** look like where you live? What can you spot around your home?

fallen leaves

sycamore seeds

After autumn it will be winter and the whole **year of seasons** begins again!

Well done!

What happens in a year?

The changes in **weather** and what happens in nature during the **seasons** are only a part of what makes a year so special.

Make a calendar for **your** year. Don't forget to include your birthday!

JANUARY

Season:

Weather:

Events:

FEBRUARY

Season:

Weather:

Events:

MARCH

Season:

Weather:

Events:

APRIL

Season:

Weather:

Events:

MAY

Season:

Weather:

Events:

JUNE

Season:

Weather:

Events:

What happens in a year?

JULY

Season:

Weather:

Events:

AUGUST

Season:

Weather:

Events:

SEPTEMBER

Season:

Weather:

Events:

OCTOBER

Season:

Weather:

Events:

NOVEMBER

Season:

Weather:

Events:

DECEMBER

Season:

Weather:

Events:

What's your favourite season?

Well done!

Get Set Go Science

Give your child a helping hand to begin learning about science.

This practical activity book will introduce your child to seasons and weather – what to expect from each season, how the weather influences seasons and why the weather changes at all. Simple explanations, colourful illustrations and wipe-clean pages mean the activities can be repeated again and again.

Wipe-clean activities to try

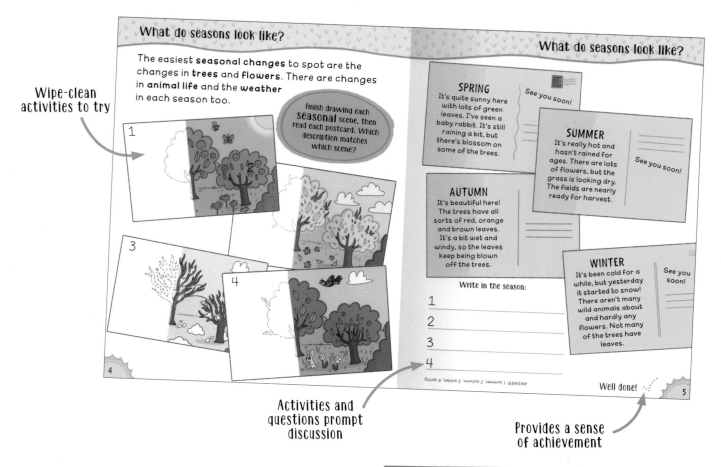

What do seasons look like?

The easiest **seasonal changes** to spot are the changes in **trees** and **flowers**. There are changes in **animal life** and the **weather** in each season too.

Finish drawing each **seasonal** scene, then read each postcard. Which description matches which scene?

1

3

4

4

What do seasons look like?

SPRING
It's quite sunny here with lots of green leaves. I've seen a baby rabbit. It's still raining a bit, but there's blossom on some of the trees.

See you soon!

SUMMER
It's really hot and hasn't rained for ages. There are lots of flowers, but the grass is looking dry. The fields are nearly ready for harvest.

See you soon!

AUTUMN
It's beautiful here! The trees have all sorts of red, orange and brown leaves. It's a bit wet and windy, so the leaves keep being blown off the trees.

WINTER
It's been cold for a while, but yesterday it started to snow! There aren't many wild animals about and hardly any flowers. Not many of the trees have leaves.

See you soon!

Write in the season:

1
2
3
4

ANSWER: 1 summer, 2 autumn, 3 winter, 4 spring

Well done!

5

Activities and questions prompt discussion

Provides a sense of achievement

ISBN 978-1-78989-068-6

Illustrated by Ellie O'Shea
Written by Emma Ranade
Concept by Fran Bromage
Designed by Simon Lee and Joe Jones
Copyright © 2020 Miles Kelly Publishing Ltd
Harding's Barn, Bardfield End Green, Thaxted,
Essex, CM6 3PX, UK. All rights reserved

Printed in China, May 2020, GSSS20

UK £5.99/US $7.95

www.MilesKelly.net

9 781789 890686

Author
Emma Ranade

fab science

TITLES IN THIS SERIES:
Animal Life • Everyday Material
Plants • Seasons and Weather

Contents

This book covers the following topics:

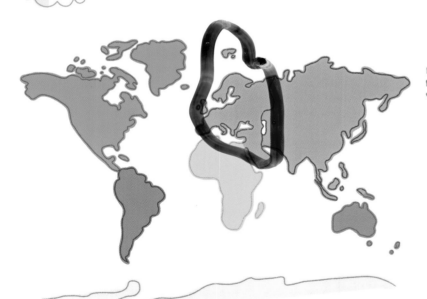

Circle the **continent** where you live. What is the weather like where you are today?

North America
South America
Europe
Africa
Asia
Oceania

Today, the weather is:

cloudy

Well done!

What do seasons look like?

The easiest **seasonal changes** to spot are the changes in **trees** and **flowers**. There are changes in **animal life** and the **weather** in each season too.

Finish drawing each **seasonal** scene, then read each postcard. Which description matches which scene?

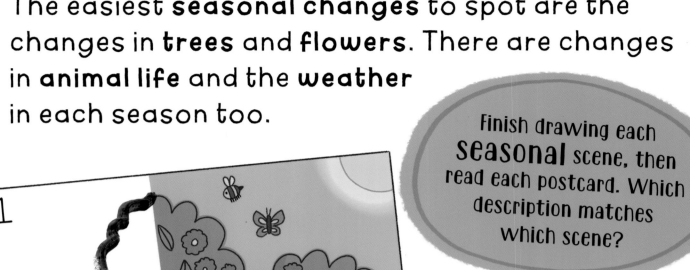